STREET PEOPLE TALES

Betsy A. Riley

BLUE DRAGON PRESS
MARYLAND

Published by Blue Dragon Press
visit our website at **www.bluedragonpress.com**

ISBN-10: 0983735697
ISBN-13: 978-0983735694 (Blue Dragon Press)

DEDICATION

Dedicated to Nancy, Sara, and Deanne,
and the members of the Poetry groups on the
AARP Community Forum, especially: LDoone,
Junduldulao, Alexdejesus, Lion, Flueln, Darksong,
Alharris, Minimickey, Snuzcook, Jen43, and Zil

CONTENTS

Street Dancer	1
Aggie	3
Phyllis	4
One-Eyed Jack	6
Seamstress Sara	7
Lady Mary	9
Tiny Kim	12
Aggie's Lost Her Marbles	14
Gardener George	16
R-R-Ralph	18
LaQuisha	20
Don Henry	22
Tammy Jo	24
Rosita	26
Recycle Michael	27
Dan the Man	28
Tommy	29
Crazy Willie	30
Tracey	32
Hector	34
Billy and Reggie	35

STREET DANCER

He dances down the street
to the music in his head
the concert never stops until
he's sound asleep in bed

Even when he sits to eat
his feet still keep the time
all he listens for is rhythm
with no heed to words or rhyme

He doesn't hear the traffic
or shouts or angry words
for the music in his head
is all he's ever heard

He eats down at the mission
then heads back to the street
and till the day he dies
he'll be dancing to the beat

AGGIE

Aggie fills her shopping cart
with treasures that she finds
assorted bits and pieces
that have value in her mind

The empty cold cream jar she found
is a lovely shade of blue
and the unmatched cup and saucer
have just a chip or two

Once she found a silver spoon
without a single scratch
no matter that her fork is steel
or that the two don't match

Her denim vest's a bit too big
but Aggie won't complain
its pockets hold the treasures
her cart cannot contain

Some old-time metal bottle caps
that remind her of her youth
some pretty stones, a bit of chalk
with which she writes the truth

Though she has other valuables
in places where she hides
her random bits of beauty
are always by her side

PHYLLIS

Phyllis runs the clinic
counting out the daily pills
the staff there like to tease her
and call her "Dr. Phyl"

She looks out for her people
and worries when they're late
she knows that if they disappear
she'll never know their fate

She softly pats each grimy hand
and offers tea and toast
but her gentle conversation
is what they value most

Phyllis greets each one by name
combined with Miss or Mister
she feeds them pride thus, eye-to-eye
in honor of her sister

Young Misty's schizophrenia
was in control for years
her family saw her smiling
but no one saw her fears

Tired of feeling frozen
Misty stopped her meds
and when her demons came to call
one midnight Misty fled

So Phyllis helps the homeless
and studies each new face
waiting for a recognition
to solve her own cold case

RECYCLE MICHAEL

Recycle Michael is rolling his cart
he doesn't just sort trash, with him it's an art
compacting the cans has a magical touch
just watch his big boots as they stomp, flip, and crush

Aluminum circles soon glint in the sun
as they fly to his cart, perfect catch every one
while he gathers his cargo he puts on a show
then trades cans for cash past the old Stop-N-Go

It's said he lives nearby, but no one knows where
he drops off his cart and melts into the air
he stands quite immobile till glances move on
then when you look back he is totally gone

His pay can't be much, only pennies a day
but it is honest work and he does it his way
his clothes may be ragged, but they're always clean
how he does his laundry, nobody has seen

ONE-EYED JACK

If you wanna hear some war tales
go see one-eyed Jack
you'll find him near the steak house
in the alleys 'round the back

Everyone knows he's a veteran
of what, he never tells
but there's glory in his stories
and man, he tells them well

Sometimes they're set in jungles
and sometimes desert sands
he praises all the fallen men
and tells of their last stands

The VA pays his room rent
but he can't stand the walls
as soon as he awakens
he's rolling down the halls

He loves those charcoal breezes
their fragrance takes him back
to days when he was tall and strong
and known as simply Jack

But don't jump to conclusions
as Jack rolls on down the street
it's not war, but diabetes
that took his legs and feet

SEAMSTRESS SARA

Sara's now a seamstress
instead of "Nathan's wife"
since she became a widow
she's redefined her life

She sold their fancy townhouse
and bought a studio
in its tiny crowded space
she doesn't miss him so

When Sara married Nathan
she was just a simple girl
A big man who could charm a room
Nate was her whole world

He built them an annuity
a sound financial plan
Nate put it all in stocks and bonds
she does not understand

The bank won't say why funds are down
or what she can expect
but some months bare necessities
take all her shrunken check

She looked out on the homeless
cold huddled on the grate
and felt a chill inside to know
she might soon share their fate

So she did alterations
and a custom dress or two
but she still felt the chill until
she figured what to do

Now she collects scrap clothing
from Goodwill reject bags
cuts it into sturdy squares
and sews a quilt from rags

And when each quilt is finished
Sara slips out like a ghost
to leave love where it will be found
by the ones who need it most

LADY MARY

Breakfast's bright and early
over at the Northside Home
but Mary's always up and dressed
face washed and hair fresh combed

She'll turn the potted violets
that line her window sill
and neatly sip the water
when the nurse brings in her pills

They call her Lady Mary
'cause she's so neatly groomed
and walks so slow and stately
each time she leaves her room

She bides her time till lunch is done
then to the park she flees
the bench she seeks rests like a throne
beneath the live oak trees

There Mary feeds the pigeons
and birds that come her way
she hoards her crusts and crackers
so they'll last out the day

The sounds take her back to Warsaw
and her grandpere's rooftop coops
before the days of Kristallnacht
and invading German troops

Her family fled the city
to her Aunt Naomi's farm
still all too soon each ended with
a tattoo on their arm

They took away her rosary
the day they shaved her head
so Mary used a knotted string
to say her prayers instead

She was the only Catholic in
the women's sleeping hall
but when she said her nightly prayers
they didn't mind at all

When Sobibor's escape was staged
Mary made it to the trees
running through the dappled shade
she'd never felt so free

She ran till her legs were leaden
and her feet began to bleed
spent, she wormed into the brush
and lay flat among the weeds

She could hear the searchers nearing
and was sure that she would die
but at least she'd have one last free look
at green leaves and blue sky

Now the search was all around her
she could hear the shots and screams
was it only chance that saved her
or the miracle it seemed

From the forest all around her
came a flock of woodland doves
soon her spot was double hidden
as the birds all perched above

Seeing birds sitting so calmly
searchers passed her thicket by
thinking no one could be hidden there
or the birds would surely fly

She's never told the story
never set her deeds to words
but every sunny afternoon
Lady Mary feeds the birds

ROSITA

Her mama crossed the river
to give birth on Texas soil
though border guards soon sent them back
the result was worth the toil

Rosita was a citizen
because she was born here
but her folks could not get green cards
as months stretched into years

When Rosita came of legal age
she did what her folks had ordered
with proof of birth clutched in her hand
Rosita crossed the border

She'd visit them each Sunday
from across the Rio Grande
but being near once they were gone
was more than she could stand

So she moved off from the desert
to a greener, cooler place .
but every time she feels the sun
she sees her mama's face

She's teaching Spanish to blue-eyed kids
and teaching English too
to those who got their green cards
as her folks could never do

TINY KIM

Her family name was Kweson
but she never thinks of them
they sold her to the circus
where she starred as Tiny Kim

She danced along the high wire
and paraded with the clowns
with a smile bright as her spangles
till she came crashing down

The downfall left her limping
with a ringing in her ears
but at least that hides the silence
once filled with children's cheers

With love, her circus family
would've found her a new place
but she couldn't stand the pity
she saw on every face

Now she fills in at the news stand
and at the corner store
when owners have to take a break
Tiny Kim will man the door

She smiles and waves at babies
as they go passing by
and when they laugh and clap their hands
she feels she still can fly

No one here knows the story
of how she got this way
but they forget her size and limp
when her smile lights up their day

AGGIE'S LOST HER MARBLES

Aggie's lost her marbles
all but her favorite one
"it's the one I'm named for"
she used to say in fun

Now it hangs around her neck
wrapped in a chamois cloth
Aggie knows it's magic
so she'll never take it off

She misses all the others
the reds and greens and blues
back when her Daddy bought them
she got to pick and choose

Most precious was the agate
with colors all a swirl
he told her it was special
just like his little girl

Back then she was a princess
her bed was soft as down
Sundays she ate ices
dressed in a lacy gown

How did that life vanish?
and how did she get here?
she shakes her head in wonder
until her vision clears

Tho' she may skulk in alleys
and sleep on sheets of stone
when she gazes at her aggie
the magic takes her home

Aggie's lost her marbles
save one, that may be true
but she has what she values most
she'll never trade with you

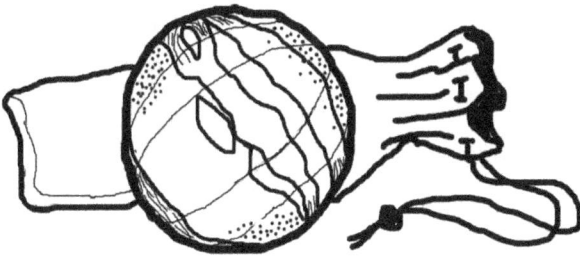

GARDENER GEORGE

He'll proudly say his name is
George Washington Carver Smith
but the magic in his fingers
is more than just a myth

He's raised night-blooming cereus
and tomato plants from seeds
but his greatest pride in growing
is the crowd his bounty feeds

He's a whiz at starting seedlings
in egg crates and tin cans
he transfers them to rooftop beds
built from scraps by his two hands

That's where Ms. Phyllis found him
when she went to grab a smoke
(she knows that she should quit now
but some days she just can't cope)

George toured her round his gardens
his heart showed in his work
his only limitations
were lack of space and dirt

So Phyllis made a leap of faith
and arranged a thoughtful gift
a key to the community garden plot
for George Washington Carver Smith

Now his zucchini crops are legend
his tomatoes in demand
so tender and so juicy
you must carry them by hand

It's a far cry from his homeless days
searching produce trash for seeds
now yuppie gardeners tip him
for his growing expertise

He grows sweet corn and carrots
and melons and green peas
all season long he hands them out
so the street folks get their C

Any time of day you'll find George
tending his garden rows
though he now has a place to sleep
home is where his garden grows

R-R-RALPH

He wanders round the outskirts
with a dustpan and a sack
scooping pavement pancakes
to sling across his back

He scrapes up cats and rabbits
and dogs and squirrels and such
the locals think he's crazy
but don't think of him much

Those who've tried to greet him
know his answer is the same
no matter what the question
"R-R-Ralph is my name"

The children laugh about him
with jokes of roadkill stew
but what he does with dead things
they haven't got a clue

He trudges round the greenbelt
till he finds the perfect spot
some days it is easy
and some days it is not

He digs a hole the perfect size
and gently lays them there
and as he covers them with earth
he mumbles a soft prayer

For the wild ones are his mission
tho' they may die alone
he's promised he will find them
and always bring them home

LAQUISHA

LaQuisha's arms are scarred by tracks
but for six months she's been clean
When she learned that she was pregnant
she quit cold and split the scene

Her first weeks were so scary
she hugged her knees and cried
until she found a well of strength
she didn't know she had inside

It was hard to break her habit
harder still to make ends meet
but she vowed to her unborn child
no more to walk the street

NA meetings at the mission
have helped her make it through
They helped her find a place to live
and work that she could do

She's cleaning office floors at night
and saving every dime
for things she knows her babe will need
when it's her birthing time

Lamaze class and yoga stretches
do more than help her thighs
as she plans a healthy baby
they're her new natural highs

She's learning to love zucchini
and do without caffeine
She'll be a grown-up mommy
although she's just a teen

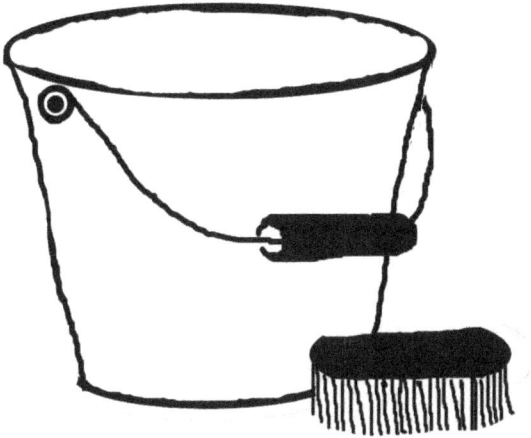

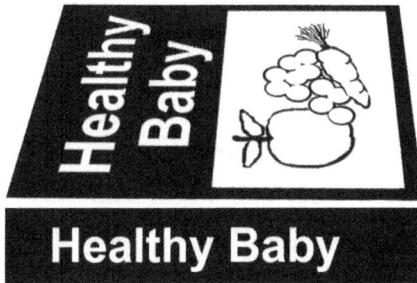

DON HENRY

You can hear Don Henry coming
by the jingling of his keys
it's a nervous affectation
that's part of his OCD

He checks the bank's computers
and several other sites
he's not much good with people
he thinks in bits and bytes

Head down, he walks and mutters
off to each job and back
his roadmap is the sidewalk
he knows each bump and crack

He never reads the street signs
or looks folks in the eyes
when Tiny Kim smiled up at him
it took him by surprise

Don's used to knowing people
by their voices and their shoes
he never thought a pixie girl
would stand right in his view

When she gave his change in nickels
and whispered with a wink
"they'll make a pretty jingle"
he felt his face turn pink

But as he hurried off to work
her words stayed in his mind
he couldn't say her tone of voice
was anything but kind

Then for the first time in his life
as he juggled password files
his pocket nickels jingled
and Don Henry cracked a smile

Now he waits to buy his paper
just when Kim is in the stand
and he's learning not to flinch
when she drops nickels in his hand

Don Henry's started healing
more than Kim will ever know
she's weaning him to people
and some day he'll say hello

TAMMY JO

Tammy Jo's mom cursed her
called her tramp and whore
so she became what she was called
till she could stand no more

When her step-dad used to beat her
Tammy never could fight back
but when he shook her baby boy
she found the strength she'd lacked

Her baby's daddy was a driver
on small town red dirt tracks
when he left, Tammy waved and cried
but he never did look back

With no one there to hold her
and no reason left to stay
she grabbed what she could call her own
and quietly slipped away

Now Tammy's in the city
to start her life anew
with just her and her baby boy
that she named Sonny Blue

She's learning not to listen
to voices from her past
and building her own self respect
as her baby grows so fast

She works hard at the diner
saving all her tips for school
so when her son is older
he'll know his mom's no fool

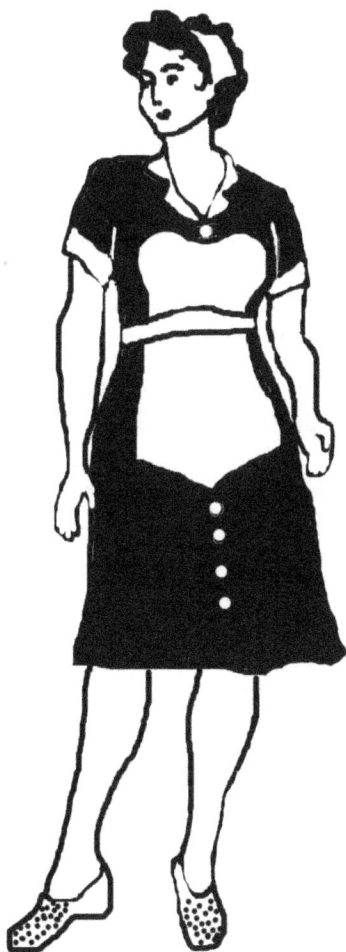

DAN THE MAN

Daniel took retirement after
thirty on the street
he doesn't have a badge or gun
but he still walks his beat

The street folk all respect him
to them he's "Dan the Man"
he can't always protect them
but he'll do what he can

He'll stop to chat with One-eyed Jack
and wave at Tiny Kim
help Lady Mary cross the street
(her eyesight's getting dim)

He does his checks on Aggie
from half a block away
she's still afraid of people
and is apt to run away

To check on Crazy Willie
Dan listens for the sounds
Will's masterful orations
can be heard for blocks around

The girls know he will walk them home
when they work late at night
They all tell Dan their troubles
and he tries to make things right

TOMMY

Tommy loves the Franken-skateboard
that he rescued from the trash
sure, he'd like to own a new one
but he'll never have the cash

Times are hard at his place
some days they can't all eat
they'd never spare a dollar
to speed his flying feet

It took months for him to scrounge
all the pieces that he needed
and he never once suspected
that Dan had interceded

Now Tommy does deliveries
for the businesses on Dale
steakhouse meals and headache pills
reach their buyers without fail

The errands are erratic
for days there'll be no trips
some customers are stingy
and give him nickel tips

But he loves the feel of flying
as he hustles down the streets
and he knows the little bits he earns
help ensure his family eats

CRAZY WILLIE

Will remembers every word
he ever has heard said
he barely learned to read and write
but he's volumes in his head

He's always spouting Shakespeare
it's his local claim to fame
he's crazy for the Avon bard
that's how he got his name

A flourish of his patchwork quilt
says the play's about to start
and how he dons his "costume"
is a clue to the star part

He drapes it like a toga
to do "et tu, Bruté"
and knots it tight around his waist
to do "the Scottish play"

Will never starts a problem
when his feet are on the ground
but when he climbs a monument
Dan has to talk him down

When Willie is performing strong
the street folk all draw near
when he does "band of brothers"
Dan and Jack both shed a tear

Crazy Willie's park orations
are the best you've ever heard
the way he pours the words out
ensures that hearts are stirred

TRACEY

Tracey waits on tables
at the steak house down on Dale
her hours are long and wages low
but she shows up without fail

She checks her daytime people
as she crosses through the park
and says a silent prayer for those
who hide till after dark

She brings bread saved from yesterday
as a treat for Mary's birds
and cranes an ear for Willie
'cause she shares his love of words

She knows he'll stop by later
at the end of her last shift
to pick up meals of leftovers
each wrapped up like a gift

Will's the one who told her
Aggie will not touch red meat
So Tracey packs up fish and spuds
to go with her sweet tea

Willie's not so picky
'bout the meals that bear his name
whether beef or fish or chicken
he likes them all the same

The owner turns a blind eye
to Tracey's giving ways
because she brings in business
with her ever smiling face

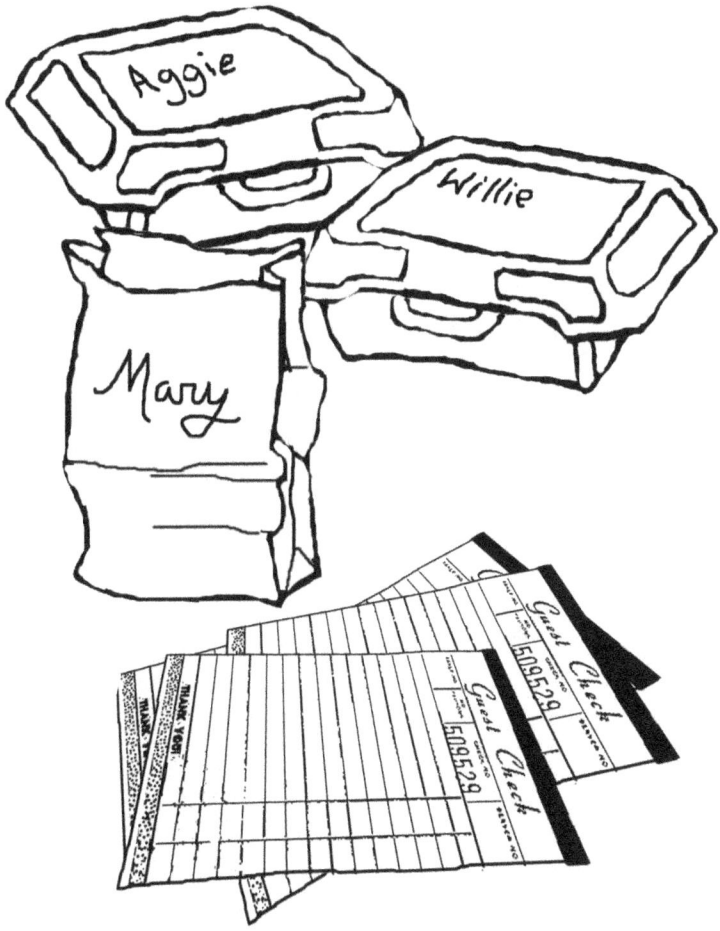

Hector

He calls himself a waiter
but that's not the whole tale
'tween gigs he busses tables at
the steakhouse down on Dale

When he serves at banquets
his red jacket feels so fine
he strides in like a matador
holding high the tray of wine

But lately he's been nervous
about voices that he hears
they're like a steady stream of thought
whispering in his ears

They tell him he should do things
a good boy would never do
and cite confusing reasons
till he's not sure what is true

He is sure that someone's watching
and feels danger to his life
so he sought out self-protection
and bought a long slim knife

BILLY & REGGIE

Since lawyer Billy lost his way
he's been living on the street
and the one that keeps him going
is his best friend on four feet

Reggie is a shepherd
who has seen better days
but now that he has Bill to love
they both will be okay

Bill walked out on his practice
after fate destroyed his life
for years he's battled nightmares
of freed perps with bloody knives

Billy couldn't face the tragedy
that took away his wife
until he bonded with the dog
he saw no good in life

Now he stands a little straighter
with less shaking in his hands
he has no words to thank the dog
but Reggie understands

Billy's slowly getting stronger
as the nightmares start to fade
one day soon he'll have the courage
to volunteer at Legal Aid

36

ABOUT THE AUTHOR

BETSY A. RILEY spends her days making the world a better place by applying supercomputing resources to science and technology research. Evenings and weekends she uses her creative talents to entertain others, spreading dreams of hope and joy.

She lives happily in Damascus, Maryland, with her husband Ken.

Betsy A. Riley

www.ingramcontent.com/pod-product-compliance
Lightning Source LLC
Chambersburg PA
CBHW030308030426
42337CB00012B/640